To: Richard

#4

CATCH & HOLD

CONTENTS

THE CATCH: A TRIBUTE

On September 10, 2005, University of Alabama
football wide receiver, Tyrone Prothro, made a
catch so extraordinary that it has gone down in
history remembered simply as The Catch. It would
earn Tyrone ESPN's 2006 ESPY award for play of
the year. When ESPN listed the greatest catches of
all time, The Catch came in at number eight, the
highest ranked college play on the list. The Catch
was no fluke. It was one great play among many for
Tyrone, yet it does stand out as something rare and
magical. When people watch it in slow motion,
they respond with laughter, scratching their heads,
and asking, "How did he *do* that?"

The University of Southern Mississippi was leading 21 to 10 with 29 seconds left in the first half. Bama was at USM's 43 yard line. On 4th and 12, Alabama quarterback Brodie Croyle took the snap in the shotgun. Tyrone went deep, and to give himself time, Brodie dropped back almost to the Bama 45, setting up for a Hail Mary pass of more than 50 yards. He threw it long with a high arch.

Tyrone was under the heaviest coverage by Jasper Faulk, one of the fastest, toughest defenders in college football, and they were moving down the field at full speed. They were approaching the goal line so close together they were bumping and pushing off each other. Tyrone saw the ball coming. Jasper realized it was coming and turned to face Tyrone, putting his body directly between Tyrone and the path of the ball.

Tyrone reached for the ball around Jasper's body, extending one arm under Jasper's left arm and the other over his right shoulder. He caught the ball behind Jasper's back and held onto it, bear-hugging Jasper to keep the ball. They tumbled to the ground, flipped and rolled, but Tyrone held the ball. Tyrone fell on his back and twisted up onto his helmet, bearing much of the weight of his body as well as Jasper's, but he kept the ball. He twisted over, Jasper rolled out of his arms, and Tyrone stood, ball in hand. He showed the ball to the referee.

The initial ruling on the field was incomplete, but after review, the pass was ruled complete and down at the 1 yard line. This set up an easy touchdown, turning the momentum of the game, which Alabama would go on to win 30-21.

In the weeks following, The Catch would be replayed hundreds of times on television. Several artists would do paintings titled The Catch, and prints of those paintings would list among the best selling in Alabama football history. It was the middle of his junior season, and Tyrone was a living legend. The NFL would snatch him up, probably before his senior year. Nothing stood in the way of him achieving the promise of his nick-name, "Pro."

Two weeks after making The Catch, in one of the most gruesome accidents in the history of televised sports, Tyrone broke both major bones in his leg between the knee-cap and ankle. As a player, he would never return to the game.

FORWARD
by Rhett Ellis

Tyrone Prothro played football with a joy that was rare but obvious at a glance. Like Ray Charles making music or Joe Dimaggio swinging a baseball bat, he did what he did for love, and the fans loved him for it.

Watching for Tyrone was like playing *Where's Waldo*. He could pop up anywhere on the field in an instant and be doing just about anything. When a big play was needed, he was the go-to man. Like many an arm-chair quarterback, I was constantly yelling for Alabama to give it to Prothro. The Catch would earn Tyrone the ESPN ESPY award for best play of the year and that was against several professional plays from several sports.

Tyrone's accident was painful, even sickening to watch. The fact that he was who he was doubled the heartbreak. Fans literally cried in the stands, in sports bars, in their homes. The following Monday, conversations around Alabama water coolers centered on whether he would come back– If anyone could, he could, everyone agreed, but that sure was a bad break.

The two events, The Catch and the accident, got connected in many fans' minds. Taken together, they were like plot points in a Shakespearean tragedy– a man rises to the top, a man loses it all.

When we met, I quickly realized that Tyrone's off-field reality was even greater than his on-field persona. With a disarming smile, here was a young man of deep humility, persistent hope, and profound honesty. The intriguing thing about the plot of his life is that in tragedy he lost nothing at all.

Introduction

Tyrone Prothro

I knew that my experiences were unusual. ESPN was playing my catch over and over, people were laughing about it, but even before the novelty of it had worn off, I was in the hospital with a broken leg.

What I then found more unusual was the way people reacted to me. I planned to come back of course, but in Division 1 college football, the loss of, say, three-tenths of a second over forty yards means you're out of the game. I tried to come back, but the simple physicality of the situation ruled it out. When I remained me through it all–same happy-go-lucky guy– people looked at me as if I were crazy or extra-spiritual or both.

I asked myself why I wasn't as messed up as everyone thought I should have been. Was I that different? I thought it over, found a few answers, and this short book is the result of my reflections. If what I do works, I want to share it.

This book is mostly about success in one's inner-life. If you're happy inside, you're happy. If you're not, you're not.

I hope you will find here a few words of encouragement, help, and maybe some hope.

Huddle Up

What they call *The Catch* was by no means an individual thing. It started in a huddle.

Watching it in reverse order, you see the quarterback, Brodie Croyle, make a fifty yard throw that put the ball right in my hands. Even if my arms happened to be wrapped around my defender, the ball was where it was supposed to be, a well-thrown Hail Mary pass. In order for Brodie to make the pass, he had to have time, and the line gave it to him. The center had to make a good snap to start the play right, and the center does what he does knowing that in less than a second after doing it, he's going to get hit hard by a two-hundred and fifty pound defensive player.

The web that enabled me to make The Catch started on the field but ran onto the sidelines to the coaching staff, the trainers, the cheerleading team. It ran into the stands to the band, the flag and dance teams and to the all-important fans. Beyond the stadium the web ran to coaches from the past, to friends, to family, and beyond.

Life's best plays start in a huddle. When I say huddle,
I don't mean networking. When I hear people talking
about networking, it sounds like they're talking about
users coming together to use each other. That's not
what I mean at all, and I wonder if networking really
works. A huddle is an entertwined structure of true
hearts joined to true hearts. A huddle could form
around the pursuit of a common passion, a religious
belief, or work, but somehow love gets in the mix. If
there's no love in it, it's not a good huddle.

I was reared in a single parent home, and my mom is my strongest connection. I have a sister and two brothers. We were so poor once that for a few nights one winter all five of us slept in the same bed with one electric heater in the room, the only heat source in the house. Now that's a huddle! My grandmothers helped raise us, and they are also at the core of my life.

Church was an early extension of our huddle. Our church was the kind where people hugged each other freely, felt free to express their emotions, and were just free in general. It was a place of healing in our community, and at any time I can close my eyes and hear the singing, see the smiles, and feel the love.

Some parts of my web just happened, but others took some effort. I believe anyone can build a web. There are times when we all feel disconnected, but no matter what, there are a few simple steps that will build a strong web. I believe anyone can do it.

The first step is a stop. There is one thing that, if we're doing it, it will prevent us from ever building a web, and in time will destroy us. If we're doing it, we have to stop, and that one thing is pursuing the love of people who for whatever reason are not inclined to love us. I played ball with young men who were desperate to be loved, usually by their fathers, and it was not there for them. No matter how well they played, there was a sadness and desperation about them. Much could be said about this, but it is not within the scope of this book. The main thing is to stop wasting time, energy, and life on something that just isn't there for the taking.

The second step is to take yourself public. You've got to get out there and get involved. Beyond my family, church, and community, it was and is sports and the numerous social activities surrounding sports for me. The opportunities to build a web are too numerous to count, but take the hobby of dancing: You can ballroom dance or square dance, river dance, line dance, or break dance. There's jazz, tap, and ballet, and there are dance clubs and assocations all over. When people get involved with a common activity that activity becomes a lens to seeing each others' souls and a mirror to seeing themselves. A fellowship forms. The teams I

played for over the years had a way by seasons' end of becoming brotherhoods, and to this day many of my best friends are my team mates.

The third step is a three-in-one: relax, smile, and just let it happen. Be open. Be real, and a huddle will form around you. The effort will come in the management of it. We have to keep our friendship list strong, and we have to do our part in each relationship.

Step four is connecting your connections to each other. Just having a circle of friends isn't having a web. A web has to connect at many points. Each person in your huddle knows that the huddle is as much theirs as it is yours. Everyone connects to everyone else. A well maintained web will grow and strengthen on its own.

Before you play, huddle up!

Run

Running is what puts you where you need to be to catch what you want to catch. In football, it's the one who accelerates into the open spaces who catches the passes.

Growing up, I loved to run. I ran track in high school, the one-hundred and two-hundred meter, and anchored the four-by-one-hundred meter relay. Each event had its own feel. The hundred meter was all intensity. You had to take off like a rocket. The two hundred was also intense, but it required endurance. Once you get more than half way, it's all about keeping your legs pumping, pushing yourself to keep accelerating, forcing yourself against the wind. Sweat covers your body. You feel you can't breathe hard enough. Taking the baton on the relay, being careful not to drop it while moving at sprint speed, was as much fun as it was a challenge.

On the football field, I was known for cuts and turns. The ability to make fast direction changes was one advantage of being a little guy on the field. I loved the way running made my leg muscles extend. I loved the feeling of overcoming resistance, finding holes in the defense, and moving the ball forward.

When I broke my leg, which became infected following surgery, losing the ability to run as I always had was among the greatest of losses, but I never stopped running in my heart. I was and always will be a runner. Some people run on their feet. Others use a bicycle

to lessen the impact on their joints. Still others run by swimming, doing step aerobics, or mountain climbing. It's all about moving at an intense and challenging pace, and there is life in it. Runners sleep better, digest their food better, live longer, and feel better.

Of equal importance with taking care of your body by exercising, I want to encourage you to move quickly to where you want to be in life. Hesitation and indecision steal time, and to lose time is to lose life. It is not the most gifted who succeed; it is those who have a clear vision of where they want to go and push themselves every day to get there.

Want to change careers? Get on the internet now and start researching educational opportunities. Dream of writing a book? A pencil and a piece of paper is all it takes to get going. Want to play in a band? Call up your buddies and set a time for your first rehearsal!

As I write this, the phenomenon of Susan Boyle is unfolding. At forty-seven years old, she took an opportunity to fulfill a dream to become a professional singer by appearing on a talent show. In a matter of days after her audition, her name was known throughout the world, a rise from obscurity to the highest level of fame and a chance to do what she loves to do.

Now, this is not to say that every dream will come true in the way we think it must, but trying definitely beats doing nothing. Your book might not reach number one on Amazon.com, but it might sell a couple hundred copies. Your band might not fill up stadiums, but you might get a gig on the deck of a beach restaurant, and what could be more fun? Another degree might not make you a C.E.O., but you could get a raise or move into a more fulfilling job.

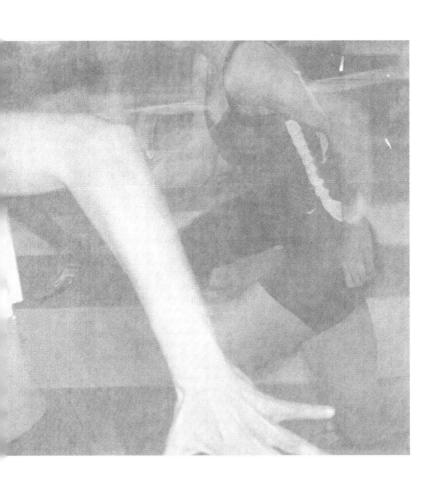

A better journey is there for the taking for those willing to get going. It is there, and it calls to us: Don't walk. Run!

Jump

Leap of faith, make the jump, a giant leap, these are expressions synonymous with risk-taking. To make the big catch, you often have to make the big jump. At my peak, my vertical leap was thirty-eight inches. At five foot, nine and a half inches tall, I could dunk a basketball. I loved to jump. I remember in tenth grade, the first time I dunked a basketball, I could not stop smiling. I had to do it again immediately, and after that it was impossible to walk past a basketball goal without wanting to dunk.

When playing football, I liked the feeling of catching a ball at the apex of a jump, way up in the air, over the heads of the big guys, and that is exactly what I was doing when I broke my leg. Do I regret making that leap? Not even one little bit. If I had not been one to take that kind of risk, I might not have broken my leg, but I definitely would not have made The Catch.

Garth Brooks recorded a song called *The Dance*. It's a song about lost love, and the conclusion of the chorus goes, "Our lives are better left to chance. I could have missed the pain, but I'd have had to miss the dance." The regret associated with taking risks seldom if ever equals the regret of not taking risks, even if that risk is love itself.

This is not to say that anyone should take foolish, uncalculated, or impulsive risks. I spent years training to make good jumps, hours lifting weights to build up my legs. The hardest part is knowing which risks are worth taking, but there are a few practical steps.

One is to get all the wise counsel you can from experienced sources who will tell you what you *need* to hear instead of what you *want* to hear. I have a few trusted friends to whom I turn when I am making decisions, and I also look to my elders. Wisdom rests under white hair. If the people who love you and have knowledge of a subject are agreeing in their advice to you, even if it is advice you do not want to hear, you had better heed it anyway.

The second step is asking yourself what is your controlling emotion? Is fear making your decisions? If so, banish fear and do the opposite of what fear is telling you. Is wounded ego, pride, or greed making your decisions? Even risks that seem competent and wise based on these motivations should not be taken. Such risks have a way of turning on you, hurting you in the end, never fulfilling whatever seemed to be promised. Is a risk all about love for you, the passion of your life, the thing that makes you want to be alive? That's a risk worth taking!

The last step is to get money as far out of the equation as possible. Take the case of a father who is picking between two jobs. One job pays twice as much as the other, but it is doing something he does not enjoy. The other would barely pay the bills, but he loves the work. He could take the high paying job and tell himself that he is doing it for his children's sake, but what kind of father would he be to them working a job he hates? In the mornings at breakfast, what would be his mood, and how would that make his children feel? In the evenings, would he come home with plenty of energy ready to have some fun with his kids, or would he be an emotionally distant, angry dad? Would making less money make a man's children love him less? Of course not. An emotional well and available father, on the other hand, is a treasure of infinite value. No matter what risk you are weighing, you have to minimize money in the decision.

There are many songs celebrating jumping. There is Van Halen's *Jump*, Kris Kross's *Jump Jump*, and House of Pain's *Jump Around*. If you want to live, truly live, you've got to jump.

Catch

Catching is a matter of finesse. If a ball is coming toward you, and you try to catch it too sharply, it will bounce off your hands, but if you are too delicate in bringing it in, it will fly through your arms. If you squeeze it too tightly it will pop right out of your hands, but if you don't hold it tight enough, it will fall at your feet. Strength, speed, and size can all be helpful with catching, but more than anything else, catching an object in motion is about a balanced touch.

You have to work with a ball's momentum. One of the most satisfying catches in football is when you are running straight down the field, and the quarterback throws it just ahead of you. You bring your speed up to the speed of the ball. As the ball comes down, it lands in your hands so perfectly that it doesn't even feel like it is moving when you bring it in to your chest.

On a cold winter day when it's below freezing and you're receiving a high punt, even if you call for the fair catch, bringing the ball in requires enough blunt force that it stings your hands.

When the air is damp and the ball is wet, you really have to be careful how you handle it. An overly tight grip will cost you possession. The key is constant calibration. Even during the split second between

the moment your hands make contact with the
ball and the moment it is safely tucked under your
arms, you have to feel your way through a series of
adjustments.

If the ball is wobbling in the air, you have to grab it at just the right moment, at just the right place on the ball, from just the right angle so that it doesn't go flipping off your arms. If the ball is in a tight spiral, you have to slow its spin as you bring it in so that it doesn't drill right through your hands.

So it is with catching anything in life. Try grabbing anything too quickly or too hard, and it will slip right through your hands. Reach for something too lightly, and the effect is the same. Imagine what it would be like if someone tossed you an expensive piece of China.

I can't imagine why someone would do that, but suppose someone did. Catching it would not be a matter of strength or power. It would be all about a delicate yet firm gripping, a gathering in of the object's momentum, a following of its arc in the air.

This principle is true of human relationships as well. In romantic relationships, if one partner doesn't hold the other tight enough or the one partner holds the other too tightly, it smothers the life out of the relationship. Some parents hold little or no authority over their

children, guaranteeing that their children will be un-
disciplined and doomed to the common mistakes of
youth. Other parents guarantee that their children will
rebel by being over-protective and over-controlling.

In negotiating, if you try too hard, you lose the deal, but if you don't try hard enough, you won't have an opportunity to make a deal.

Finesse is largely a matter of practice. You have to get the hang of a thing, the feel of it. The things we do best are those things we have done so many times that we don't even have to think about what we are doing. Watching a pizza chef toss and spin dough, it would be easy to think, "Wow, what a talent he was born with," but he had to start at the beginning, perhaps with very little inborn talent, and learn the feel of the dough, learn just the right speed to spin it, just the right height to toss it, just the right touch to catch it on its way back down.

If you try too hard to be the life of the party, you will be an obnoxious bore. On the other hand, if you stand off and refuse to be sociable, you won't get invited back. Try too hard for a job, and the employer will pass on you, but act like you don't care whether you get the job, and the outcome will be the same.

In the push and pull of life, in almost every category of life, it is finesse that makes the catch.

Keep Holding On

Unless you are already in the end-zone, once you catch the ball, you have to move it down the field. To do that, you have to tuck it in and hold on tight.

I would like to say to those who are in discouraging circumstances, just keep holding on.

When I was in fifth grade, our house burned down. There we were, dirt poor and struggling, but Mama kept us alive, kept us going. After something like that, I guess losing my chance to play professional football didn't seem so devastating. Even so, I never gave up on my football dreams. Though I could not be on the field, my heart stayed in the game. At the time of this writing I am on the coaching staff of a semi-professional football team. I'm still in the game, still holding on.

Are you a mother or father, doing everything in your power to raise good kids? Keep holding on. One day when you watch your children walk across the stage to receive their diplomas, you will know in your heart that it was worth it, and you will know, even if no one else in the world knows, how you held on. If your children don't finish school, keep holding on. Even if a child of yours gets addicted to drugs or sentenced to time in jail, keep holding on. There is light at the end of all tunnels. And if, tragedy of all tragedies, you have lost a child, keep holding on to the hope that you will see that child fully restored someday in the presence of God.

Are you working your way through college, waiting tables or delivering pizza in hopes of becoming a teacher someday? A nurse? A doctor? Keep holding on. The first time you teach a struggling student to

read or do long division, it will be worth it. The first time you treat a burn victim or perform a life saving heart surgery in just the nick of time, it will be worth it. Keep holding on.

One of the most succesful films in history is Rocky. Sylvester Stallone wrote Rocky after repeated failed attempts to make it as an actor. His own character was mirrored in Rocky Balboa, the hero of the film, and what made Rocky unique and powerful was the ending. The hero lost the fight.

It was not about winning. It was about standing. Rocky went the distance. He stayed on his feet until the last bell sounded. That is the definition of hero. What Stallone did in real life by holding on to his dream when the odds were increasingly against him was the very thing portrayed in the movie, heroism.

We are human, and we are limited, but in this life, there are millions of ways to manifest that which is divine.

More than anything else, my part in The Catch was just to keep holding on. Sometimes that's all a person can do. Keep holding on.

You can contact Tyrone Prothro at proth0204@yahoo.com. His website is www.tyroneprothro.com.

LaVergne, TN USA
25 October 2009
161843LV00002B/1/P